Aral Silversong's Spells and Curses for Beginner Sorcerers

Lara Paschke

BookLeaf Publishing

Presentation by *BookLeaf Publishing*

Web: www.bookleafpub.com

E-mail: info@bookleafpub.com

ISBN: 9789357617741

First edition 2022

Dedicated to all my MAGICAL teachers over the years, who have helped me with my poetry and English skills. (Especially Mrs. Elliott, my Year Four teacher, who I promised my first book dedication to! Thank you Mrs. Elliott)

ACKNOWLEDGEMENT

Although, I could have used my magic powers to edit this book, making it come to life and edit itself, I thought it would be much better to spend some quality time with my Mum! I'd really like to thank her for helping my poetry skills. I really couldn't have done it without you, thank you Mum! <3 I also would like to thank Book Leaf Publishing for hosting this fantastic challenge - I had so much fun writing the poems, and now I'm a published author!

PREFACE

WARNING! Some of the spells and curses in this book hold extreme power and are VERY DANGEROUS. Only Sorcerers who wield power can perform these - recommended for unexperienced beginners. (No reactions guaranteed)

A Quick Introduction...

Open the pages and take a look,
At the magic throughout this book.
The Spells are good and free to use,
Whereas with Curses, you would generally lose.

But don't feel any bit shy,
For this magic won't let you die,
Because as I stated just before,
And as I'll probably say a little bit more,
There is absolutely no reaction guaranteed.

Cleaning Spell (Bilobess)

Dusty shelves,
And messy rooms,
Here comes the magic broom.

Dirty tables,
Littered toys,
Use this spell with lots of noise!

"Shopnopdelirits,
I call the spirits.
Bilobess,
Please clean up this mess!"

(WARNING. This spell won't work if you don't say "please")

Bully Curse (Gullonmables)

Teases and Tricks,
Can do lots of harm.
But you can stop it with this charm.

When someone's getting bullied,
Day or night,
Cast this Curse, with no fright.

"Shopnopdelex,
I conjure this hex.
Gullonmables
It's time to turn the tables."

Use this curse with care,
And turn the tables if you dare.
The bully's tricks, teases and taunts,
Will get them back and will forever haunt.

Summoning Charm

A wink of an eye,
Hold out your hand.
Imagine an object -
It'll come to your command.

Storm Spell (Rainopex)

Clapping thunder,
Striking lightning.
All of this is very frightening.

Clouds of grey,
Lights of yellow.
When you cast this spell, you must bellow.

"Shopnopdelirits,
I call the spirits.
Rainopex,
Volume alters the effects."

Time Spell (Thymeldee)

It can be hard
To travel time,
Yet, say no more, just read this rhyme.

It's not too complicated,
As you'll see.
Just please do follow these rules of three.

First, not last,
Avoid yourself in the past.
Next – once cast,
The magic won't forever last.
And finally, I come to three.
Whatever done can effect present you and me.

"Shopnopdelirits,
I call the spirits.
Thymeldee,
Close your eyes and count to three!"

Transformation Curse (Ackortangers)

Close your eyes,
Please quite tight -
And imagine an object, heavy or light.

Object or animal,
This Curse is fun.
But you must be warned of the dangers to come.

If you stay out of your body for too long,
Things could go VERY wrong.

"Shopnopdelex,
I conjure this hex,
Ackortangers,
I've warned you of the dangers."

Flight Spell (Farlyreins)

Birds are flying up so high -
And you can join them in the sky.

There are no consequential tricks,
Just be warned- you must be quick.

"Shopnopdelirits,
I call the spirits.
Farlyreins,
Join the birds and planes."

Water Breathing Charm

Hold your breath,
And make this wish.
"I want to breathe
With the fish!"

Ghosting Spell (Vilobility)

The Spell to lose your visibility,
Doesn't have much liability.

But when it occasionally works,
This Spell surely has its perks.

But since when it works, it's only pure luck,
You must be sure, not to get stuck.

"Shopnopdelirits,
I call the spirits.
Vilobility,
Harness the invisibility!"

Senses Curse (Seagobadare)

When there's blurry eyes,
Or no smell,
When you cannot even hear a bell.

When a sense is gone,
If your taste is bland,
When you cannot even feel your hand.

You shall cast this Curse under a cloud,
And you'll fix your sense from those around.

"Shopnopdelex,
I conjure this hex.
Seagobadare,
Those around, must beware."

This Curse works best at night,
Under a cloud, when there's no light.

Numbing Spell (Furolaray)

When a feeling is too strong,
Or if the pain is just too long,
You can make that sense go numb,
Whether at your head or at your bum!

To take away the hurt or fear,
And make that feeling disappear,
That one emotion you once had,
Would go away and not feel bad.

"Shopnopdelirits,
I call the spirits.
Furolaray,
Make the feeling go away."

Memory Spell (Remberlime)

When you've lost a thought,
One you really ought to sought,
One that's completely lost your mind,
But your far too lazy to find.

This is the Spell that will do the trick,
It will find the thought that you can't seem to pick.

"Shopnopdelirits
I call the spirits.
Remberlime,
Let's not have a next time!"

Muting Charm

When that loud sound,
Is all too near,
Just stick your finger
In your ear.

Life Curse (Lilolamay)

Once a life has been taken away,
It can be quite sad.
But this Curse can bring them back,
So it's not too bad.

But after this Curse has been cast,
Remember YOUR life won't forever last...

"Shopnopdelex,
I conjure this hex.
Lilolamay,
Life from you is taken away."

Healing Spell (Ecorixed)

Broken bones,
Or fractured wrists,
There's no need for medical lists!

With this Spell,
You'll say no more,
Of those injuries that are quite sore.

Wave your hands
Be gentle like rain,
And then next, there is no pain!

"Shopnopdelirits,
I call the spirits,
Ecorixed,
The injuries have been fixed!"

Speed Charm

Clap your hands,
No more than twice.
Lift them up -
Your speed is thrice.

Strength Spell (Jullenorym)

When you're too lazy
To work at the gym,
But your quite jealous of that guys muscles and him.

Just cast this Spell
With a voice so strong,
And YOUR muscles will visit for long!

"Shopnopdelirits,
I call the spirits,
Jullenorym,
No need for the gym!"

Charging Curse (Grevorow)

This Curse of power can fill up your phone,
When there's no charger, anywhere at home.

It would work anywhere-
But there's something to beware.

Every time you top up a device.
It'll take from you and won't feel nice.

Eventually you'll drain from all your strength.
Would you really go to this length?

"Shopnopdelex,
I conjure this hex.
Grevorow,
Are you happy now?"

Gold Curse (Glemillah)

Sparkling yellow,
Solid gold,
Truth be told, this Curse never gets old.

After this magic,
You'll be eating golden meals.
You'll show everybody that magic is real.

But don't fill your purse too much,
Or you'll become treasure to the touch.

"Shopnopdelex,
I conjure this hex.
Glemillah,
Enjoy the treasure!"

A Wizard in Dismay

Thousands of years, and millions of days,
There was a man who lived in dismay.
But then he discovered magic,
And it had put an end to his tragic.

The newfound wizard had been glad,
To find something to not be sad.
But as time passed, he wouldn't use Charms,
He had moved onto Curses, filled with harm.

He had switched from dismay over to glad,
And then used Hexes and turned to mad.
In time, the magic drove his true self away,
And when he used Curses, he filled with dismay.

This is the warning every Sorcerer hears,
They pass it down to their friends and peers.
Don't use your magic to cause upheaval,
Or else you might find yourself turning evil.

www.ingramcontent.com/pod-product-compliance
Lightning Source LLC
Chambersburg PA
CBHW062206160726
48282CB00027B/1014
9789357617741